W9-CCE-595

950.4
DEL

De Lee, Nigel.

Rise of the Asian
superpowers from
1945

$12.90

DATE			

5/88

Palmer Public Library
655 S. Valley Way
DISCARD   99645

© THE BAKER & TAYLOR CO.

Editor: Catherine Bradley
Designer: Charles Matheson
Researcher: Cecilia Weston-Baker

Illustrated by Stefan Chabluk, Paul
Cooper and Rob Shone

© Aladdin Books Ltd 1987

Designed and produced by
Aladdin Books Ltd
70 Old Compton Street
London W1V 5PA

*First published in the
United States in 1987 by*
Franklin Watts
387 Park Avenue South
New York, NY 10016

ISBN 0-531-10407-9

Library of Congress Catalog
Card Number: 87-80229

All rights reserved

Printed in Belgium

Front cover: Chinese observers at a nuclear test explosion.